WORKB

FOR

LIMITLESS

EXPANDED EDITION

UPGRADE YOUR BRAIN, LEARN ANYTHING FASTER, AND UNLOCK YOUR EXCEPTIONAL LIFE

A Practical Workbook for Jim Kwik's book"

Jada J. Carlson

This book belongs to:

_____

_____

Disclaimer

This workbook, the "Limitless Workbook," is intended for personal development and educational purposes. The content within is designed to complement the concepts explored in the "Limitless" book by Jim Kwik, providing additional insights, exercises, and interactive elements to enhance the reader's understanding and application of the discussed principles. It is not produced, endorsed, or affiliated with the original creators, authors, or publishers of the original book.

About This Workbook

As you delve into the pages of this workbook, you'll find a carefully crafted companion to the powerful teachings of "Limitless." Each section corresponds to key themes and chapters from the book, offering practical exercises, reflection prompts, and activities to reinforce the concepts presented by Jim Kwik.

How to Use This Workbook

To maximize the benefits of this workbook, consider the following :

1. **Read "Limitless" First:** Ensure you've read Jim Kwik's "Limitless" before diving into the workbook. This workbook is designed to enhance and apply the principles from the book.
2. **Follow the Structure:** Navigate through the workbook using the provided table of contents. The sections align with the main themes in "Limitless," creating a seamless and immersive learning experience.
3. **Active Engagement:** This workbook is not meant for passive reading. Engage actively with the exercises, activities, and reflection prompts. The more actively you participate, the more profound and lasting your insights will be.
4. **Personalization:** Tailor the exercises to your unique preferences and circumstances. "Limitless" is about unlocking your individual potential, and this workbook provides a space for you to personalize the teachings to suit your needs.
5. **Note-taking:** Utilize the note-taking sections to define your objectives and outline the steps you'll take to achieve them. "Limitless" encourages actionable steps, and this workbook is your tool for translating those steps into reality.
6. **Reflect and Celebrate:** Take time to reflect on your progress and celebrate your achievements. The workbook includes dedicated sections for tracking your journey, providing a roadmap for your personal development.

Remember, this workbook is not just a companion but a dynamic tool to guide you through the process of becoming the best version of yourself. Embrace the exercises, enjoy the journey, and get ready to unleash the limitless potential that resides within you!

TABLE OF CONTENTS

INTRODUCTION

Welcome to the "Limitless" Workbook – Your Personal Guide to Unleashing Your Full Potential!

Congratulations on taking the first step toward transforming your life and unlocking the limitless capabilities within you. This workbook is designed to complement Jim Kwik's transformative book, "Limitless," providing you with a hands-on and interactive experience as you embark on a journey of self-discovery, accelerated learning, and personal growth.

Jim Kwik pointed out in his book "Limitless" that there is no such thing as a good or bad memory; there is merely a trained memory and an untrained memory.

LIMITLESS: Upgrade your brain, learn anything faster, and unlock your exceptional life

By implementing a set of practical techniques, we can boost our brainpower and learning capacity.

While there's no magical pill for genius, a well-defined process is laid out within the pages of the book "Limitless".

"Limitless" serves as a guide for enhancing not only the speed and efficiency of learning but also for nurturing your physical brain. Through practices such as nutrition, supplements, exercise, meditation, sleep, and more, the book provides a blueprint for fostering the growth of new brain cells and strengthening the connections between them.

PART I

FREE YOUR MIND

CHAPTER 1: BECOMING LIMITLESS

FUNDAMENTAL LESSONS

1. Impact of Childhood Beliefs: Jim Kwik highlights the profound impact of childhood beliefs on one's self-perception. Negative thoughts can shape behavior and limit potential, he emphasizes the need to overcome negative childhood labels that may limit personal growth.

2. External Labels Influence Self-Image: External labels, such as "the boy with the broken brain," can significantly influence an individual's self-image and behavior. This lesson underscores the need to challenge and redefine externally imposed identities to foster personal growth.

3. Mindset, Motivation, and Method: The three-part framework of becoming limitless is introduced, consisting of Mindset (beliefs and attitudes), Motivation (purpose and energy for action), and Method (specific processes for accomplishing goals). These elements collectively contribute to personal development.

4. Learning as a Superpower: Jim Kwik described Learning as a superpower, and the chapter asserts that everyone has the capacity to learn, given the right tools and mindset.

5. The Limitless Model: Individuals can become limitless in their own way by adopting the Limitless Model, which includes the three components: Mindset, Motivation, and Method.

SELF-REFLECTION QUESTIONS

1. Impact of Childhood Beliefs:
- Are there any negative thoughts or self-limiting beliefs that you still carry with you today? How have these childhood beliefs influenced your behavior and decisions in various aspects of your life?

_____

_____

_____

_____

_____

- What steps can you take to foster more positive self-talk and reshape any limiting beliefs that may be holding you back?

_____

_____

_____

_____

2. External Labels Influence Self-Image:
- Have you ever experienced external labels or judgments that influenced how you see yourself? How do external perceptions, whether positive or negative, shape your self-image and behavior?

_____

_____

_____

_____

- In what ways can you challenge and redefine external labels to foster personal growth and a more authentic self-image?

_____

_____

_____

_____

3. Coping Mechanisms and Self-Perception:
- Reflect on any coping mechanisms you may have developed in response to challenges or negative perceptions. Are these coping mechanisms helping or hindering your personal development and growth?

_____

_____

_____

_____

- What positive alternatives can you explore to replace any potentially detrimental coping strategies?

_____

_____

_____

_____

4. The Power of Learning How to Learn:

- Are you actively exploring different learning methodologies, or do you follow a more passive approach? What steps can you take to understand and apply the principles of effective learning in your life?

_____

_____

_____

_____

5. Learning as a Superpower:

- Reflect on your attitude towards learning. Do you view it as a superpower that can unlock new opportunities and potential? And In what ways can you harness the limitless ability to learn and apply effective methods and strategies for continuous growth?

_____

_____

_____

_____

_____

NOTES

CHAPTER 2: WHY THIS MATTERS NOW

FUNDAMENTAL LESSONS

1. Balancing Information Consumption: The lesson from the "Digital Deluge" is the importance of managing and balancing the intake of information. In a world inundated with data, individuals need effective strategies to navigate the constant flow of information, ensuring it doesn't lead to overwhelm and negatively impact productivity and well-being.

2. Guarding Against Digital Distractions: The "Digital Distraction" lesson highlights the need to safeguard attention in the digital age. Recognizing the allure of digital stimuli and the transient pleasure it provide, individuals should proactively cultivate focus to engage in deep relationships, meaningful learning, and concentrated work.

3. Mindful Technology Use: "Digital Dementia" underscores the importance of mindful and intentional use of digital technology. Excessive reliance on devices may lead to cognitive atrophy, impacting memory and mental capabilities. The lesson encourages individuals to strike a balance between utilizing technology and engaging their cognitive functions.

4. Preserving Critical Thinking Skills: The "Digital Deduction" lesson warns against over-relying on technology for critical thinking and reasoning. While technology is a valuable tool, there's a risk of diminishing one's ability for independent thought and analysis. The lesson encourages a mindful approach to using technology to preserve and strengthen critical thinking skills.

5. Cultivating Technological Literacy: A broader lesson from the entire passage is the importance of cultivating technological literacy. Understanding the potential pitfalls of excessive digital engagement allows individuals to make informed choices, ensuring that technology enhances rather than detracts from their overall well-being and cognitive abilities.

SELF-REFLECTION QUESTIONS

1. Balancing Information Consumption:
- How do you currently manage the influx of information in your daily life? Are there specific areas where information overload negatively impacts your productivity or well-being?

_____

_____

_____

_____

_____

- What effective strategies can you implement to navigate the constant flow of information more efficiently?

_____

_____

_____

_____

_____

2. Guarding Against Digital Distractions:
- Reflect on instances where digital distractions have affected your ability to focus on meaningful tasks. What proactive measures can you take to minimize digital distractions and cultivate sustained focus?

_____

_____

_____

_____

_____

- How can you strike a balance between the benefits of technology and the need for undivided attention in relationships, learning, and work?

_____

_____

_____

_____

_____

3. Mindful Technology Use:
- Assess your current use of digital technology. Are there areas where you may be over-relying on devices? What intentional steps can you take to ensure mindful and purposeful engagement with technology?

_____

_____

_____

_____

- In what ways can you balance the convenience of technology with maintaining your cognitive functions and mental capabilities?

_____

_____

_____

_____

_____

4. Preserving Critical Thinking Skills:
- Consider your reliance on technology for critical thinking and reasoning. Are there aspects where technology may be replacing independent thought? How can you use technology as a tool to enhance, rather than replace, your critical thinking skills?

_____

_____

_____

_____

_____

- What practices can you adopt to ensure that your analytical abilities continue to thrive in the digital age?

_____

_____

_____

_____

_____

5. Cultivating Technological Literacy:
- Reflect on your level of technological literacy and awareness of potential pitfalls in digital engagement. Are there areas where you could enhance your understanding of the impact of technology on well-being and cognitive abilities?

_____

_____

_____

_____

- How can you make informed choices to ensure that technology contributes positively to your overall life and learning experiences?

_____

_____

_____

_____

_____

NOTES

CHAPTER 3: YOUR LIMITLESS BRAIN

FUNDAMENTAL LESSONS

1. Exceptional Brain Capabilities: Your brain is an extraordinary organ with immense capabilities, generating 70,000 thoughts daily and operating at speeds surpassing the fastest computers. The lesson here is to recognize and appreciate the unparalleled potential within your brain.

2. Neuroplasticity and Lifelong Learning: Neuroplasticity allows your brain to adapt and change continually based on activities and environmental influences. Learning is not a fixed process; it involves forming new synaptic connections, demonstrating that lifelong learning can reshape your brain and unlock limitless possibilities.

3. The Significance of Gut Health: The presence of a "second brain" in your gut, known as the enteric nervous system (ENS), highlights the interconnectedness of gut health and mental well-being. Understanding the impact of nutrition on both the gut and the brain emphasizes the importance of nourishing your body for optimal cognitive function.

4. Taking Charge of Your Own Learning: Despite the brain's potential, the challenge lies in a lack of education on how to leverage it fully. Few schools globally teach the essential skill of learning how to learn. The key takeaway is the responsibility to take charge of your own education, emphasizing self-directed learning beyond what formal education provides.

5. Value in Expertise and Critical Thinking: story of the skilled technician underscores the value of expertise and critical thinking. Knowing which actions to take and making informed decisions can be more valuable than the actions themselves. This lesson encourages cultivating expertise, problem-solving skills, and critical thinking, highlighting their role in adding value to one's endeavors.

SELF-REFLECTION QUESTIONS

1. Neuroplasticity and Lifelong Learning:
- Reflect on instances in your life where learning something new led to a noticeable change in your perspective or skills. How can the concept of neuroplasticity inspire you to embrace lifelong learning and actively seek new experiences to reshape your brain positively?

_____

_____

_____

_____

2. Significance of Gut Health:
- Consider your current understanding of the connection between gut health and mental well-being. Are there changes you can make in your dietary habits to support optimal cognitive function? How might a holistic approach to well-being, including both brain and gut health, enhance your overall quality of life?

_____

_____

_____

_____

3. Taking Charge of Your Learning:
- Reflect on your educational experiences. To what extent were you taught how to learn versus what to learn?

_____

_____

_____

_____

- In what ways can you take more responsibility for your learning journey, especially in areas where formal education might be lacking?

_____

_____

_____

_____

4. Value in Expertise and Critical Thinking:
- How can you actively cultivate expertise, problem-solving skills, and critical thinking in various aspects of your life to add value to your endeavors?

_____

_____

_____

_____

5. Leveraging a Limitless Mind:
  • Reflect on the idea of a limitless mind and its potential to add value. How can you leverage your ability to think, solve problems, and innovate in your personal and professional pursuits?

_____

_____

_____

_____

  • In what ways can cultivating a mindset of continuous learning contribute to personal and financial growth?

_____

_____

_____

_____

6.The Power of Reading:
  • Consider your current reading habits. How has reading impacted your personal and intellectual growth? What changes or additions can you make to your reading habits to harness the power of this effective method for programming new ideas into your brain?

_____

_____

_____

_____

NOTES

CHAPTER 4: HOW TO READ AND REMEMBER THIS (AND ANY) BOOK

FUNDAMENTAL LESSONS

1. Forgetting Curve Awareness:
   - Understand that individuals tend to lose around 50% of newly acquired knowledge within an hour and an average of 70% within 24 hours.

2. Pomodoro Technique for Optimal Focus:
   - Embrace the Pomodoro technique, a time-management strategy, advocating 25 minutes of focused work followed by a 5-minute break for optimal productivity.

3. Impact of Primacy and Recency in Learning:
   - Appreciate the psychological phenomenon that what is learned at the beginning of a session is more likely to be remembered (primacy).

4. FASTER Method for Enhanced Learning:
   - Utilize the FASTER method (Forget, Act, State, Teach, Enter, and Review) as a structured approach to enhance learning and retention.

5. The Power of Asking Questions:
   - Understand the pivotal role questions play in memory and comprehension.
   - Acknowledge the sensory overload experienced, with the conscious mind processing only a fraction of the available information.
   - Recognize the reticular activating system (RAS) as a filtering mechanism influenced by the questions asked, guiding the brain on what is deemed important.

6. Mind Preparation Through Questions:
   - Emphasize the importance of questions in directing focus and comprehension in various aspects of life, including reading.
   - Acknowledge that a lack of questioning during reading compromises concentration, understanding, and recall.

SELF-REFLECTION QUESTIONS

1. Forgetting Curve Awareness:
   - Reflect on instances when you've experienced the forgetting curve. How did it impact your learning and retention of information?

_____

_____

_____

- What strategies have you employed in the past to counteract the effects of the forgetting curve?

_____

_____

_____

_____

2. Pomodoro Technique for Optimal Focus:
- Assess your own ability to maintain focus during tasks. Do you notice a decline in concentration after a specific duration?

_____

_____

- Have you tried the Pomodoro technique or similar time-management strategies in your work or study routine? What were the results?

_____

_____

_____

3. Impact of Primacy and Recency in Learning:
- Consider your learning experiences. Can you recall instances where information learned at the beginning or end of a session had a lasting impact?

_____

_____

_____

- How might you intentionally structure your learning sessions to leverage the primacy and recency effects for better retention?

_____

_____

_____

_____

4. FASTER Method for Enhanced Learning:
- Evaluate the FASTER method components (Forget, Act, State, Teach, Enter, Review). Which elements do you currently incorporate into your learning process?

_____

_____

_____

_____

- How might the FASTER method be applied to specific learning challenges or subjects you find challenging?

_____

_____

_____

_____

5. The Power of Asking Questions:
- Reflect on a recent reading experience. Did you consciously ask questions while reading? How did it affect your comprehension and retention? Consider a topic or subject you're currently learning. What questions could you ask to enhance your understanding and retention?

_____

_____

_____

_____

6.Mind Preparation Through Questions:
- Examine your reading habits. How often do you actively engage with the material by asking questions? In what areas of your life, beyond reading, could asking more questions contribute to improved focus, understanding, and recall?

_____

_____

_____

_____

NOTES

PART II

LIMITLESS MINDSET:
THE WHAT

CHAPTER 5: THE SPELL OF BELIEF SYSTEMS

FUNDAMENTAL LESSONS

1. Forgetting Curve Awareness:
   - Understand that individuals tend to lose around 50% of newly acquired knowledge within an hour and an average of 70% within 24 hours.

2. Pomodoro Technique for Optimal Focus:
   - Embrace the Pomodoro technique, a time-management strategy, advocating 25 minutes of focused work followed by a 5-minute break for optimal productivity.

3. Impact of Primacy and Recency in Learning:
   - Appreciate the psychological phenomenon that what is learned at the beginning of a session is more likely to be remembered (primacy).

4. FASTER Method for Enhanced Learning:
   - Utilize the FASTER method (Forget, Act, State, Teach, Enter, and Review) as a structured approach to enhance learning and retention.

5. The Power of Asking Questions:
   - Understand the pivotal role questions play in memory and comprehension.
   - Acknowledge the sensory overload experienced, with the conscious mind processing only a fraction of the available information.
   - Recognize the reticular activating system (RAS) as a filtering mechanism influenced by the questions asked, guiding the brain on what is deemed important.

6. Mind Preparation Through Questions:
   - Emphasize the importance of questions in directing focus and comprehension in various aspects of life, including reading.
   - Acknowledge that a lack of questioning during reading compromises concentration, understanding, and recall.

SELF-REFLECTION QUESTIONS

1. Self-Talk Awareness:
   - Reflect on your inner dialogue. How often does your self-talk focus on limitations and what you believe you cannot achieve? Identify instances where this voice has discouraged you from pursuing goals or desires.

_____

_____

_____

_____

2. Impact of Limiting Beliefs:
   - Consider the ways in which limiting beliefs have hindered your progress, even in areas where you generally excel. How have these beliefs influenced your actions and decisions?

_____

_____

_____

_____

3. Shifting Mindset:
   - Evaluate your mindset about personal potential. Are you inclined to believe that "things are the way they are," or do you recognize the possibility of modifying and shaping your brain to achieve objectives? Reflect on times when believing in yourself has positively impacted your achievements.

_____

_____

_____

_____

4. Thermometer vs. Thermostat Analogy:
   - Consider the analogy of a thermometer and thermostat. In what ways does your mindset resemble that of a thermometer, merely reacting to external circumstances? How might adopting a thermostat mindset, actively measuring and adjusting your environment, enhance your ability to overcome limiting beliefs?

_____

_____

_____

_____

5. Overcoming Limiting Beliefs:

Key 1: Naming Limiting Beliefs

- What negative self-talk patterns have you identified? Take time to name and acknowledge these limiting beliefs. Reflect on how recognizing them can be a crucial step toward overcoming them.

_____

_____

_____

_____

Key 2: Examining the Facts

- When examining the truthfulness of your beliefs, consider whether there is evidence to support these restrictions. Reflect on instances where cognitive biases or distorted thinking may have influenced your perception of limitations.

_____

_____

_____

_____

Key 3: Creating a New Belief

- Reflect on the process of creating a new, empowering belief. How can this new belief be both grounded in reality and beneficial to the limitless self you aspire to become? Consider the positive impact such a belief can have on your mindset and actions.

_____

_____

_____

_____

NOTES

CHAPTER 6: THE 7 LIES OF LEARNING

FUNDAMENTAL LESSONS

1. Mindset Flexibility:
   - Old Belief: Intelligence is fixed.
   - New Belief: Embrace a growth mindset; skills and intellect can be developed through hard work, effective teaching, and persistence. Your IQ is not fixed; it depends on your ability to cultivate a growth mindset.

2. Unlocking Full Brain Potential:
   - Old Belief: We only use 10 percent of our brains.
   - New Belief: Recognize the myth and affirm that you have the full power of your brain available. Adopt the belief that you are learning to utilize your entire brain in the best way possible.

3. Redefining Mistakes:
   - Old Belief: Mistakes are failures.
   - New Belief: Mistakes are not failures; they indicate an attempt at something new. Embrace the idea that life is about personal growth, not comparison with others. There is no such thing as failure; there is only failure to learn.

4. Empowering Knowledge through Action:
   - Old Belief: Knowledge is power.
   - New Belief: Challenge the notion that knowledge alone is power. Understand that knowledge gains its potential through action. Adopt the equation: Knowledge × Action = Power.

5. Learning as an Evolving Process:
   - Old Belief: Learning new things is very difficult.
   - New Belief: Shift the perspective on learning. Recognize that learning is a set of strategies, and it becomes more enjoyable and accessible when you understand how to learn. Discovering new methods to learn makes the process fun and easier.

6. Detachment from Others' Opinions:
   - Old Belief: The criticism of other people matters.
   - New Belief: Reject the significance of others' criticism in shaping your life. Take responsibility for your own self-worth and decisions. It's not your responsibility to seek approval; it's yours to like, love, and respect yourself.

7. Genius as a Developed Skill:
   - Old Belief: Genius is born.
   - New Belief: Challenge the idea that genius is innate. Embrace the concept that genius is developed through intense practice, deep learning, and expert coaching.

Understand that anyone can acquire skills that may seem like genius through deliberate practice and dedication. Genius leaves a trail of clues, and greatness is grown, not born.

SELF-REFLECTION QUESTIONS

1. Mindset Flexibility:
   - In what ways can you challenge the belief that intelligence is fixed and embrace the idea of continuous development? How can you actively cultivate a growth mindset in your daily life?

_____

_____

_____

_____

2. Unlocking Full Brain Potential:
   - Reflect on instances where you've limited yourself based on the misconception that you only use 10 percent of your brain. How can you reframe this belief to empower yourself? What steps can you take to explore and utilize your entire brain capacity more effectively?

_____

_____

_____

_____

3. Redefining Mistakes:
   - Consider instances where fear of failure held you back. How might embracing mistakes as part of the learning process impact your future actions?

_____

_____

_____

_____

4. Detachment from Others' Opinions:
   - Reflect on situations where you allowed others' opinions to influence your decisions. How might your life change if you detached from external criticism?

_____

_____

_____

_____

- Explore ways to reinforce your self-worth independently of external validation. How can you foster a stronger sense of self-approval?

_____

_____

_____

_____

5. Genius as a Developed Skill:
- Identify a skill or area where you admire someone's "genius." How might their journey of intense practice and deep learning inspire your own development?

_____

_____

_____

_____

- Reflect on a time when you achieved a level of mastery through deliberate practice. How can you apply this principle to other aspects of your life?

_____

_____

_____

_____

NOTES

PART III

LIMITLESS MOTIVATION: THE WHY

CHAPTER 7: PURPOSE

FUNDAMENTAL LESSONS

1. SMART Goal Setting:
Setting SMART goals (Specific, Measurable, Actionable, Realistic, and Time-based) is an effective strategy for achieving objectives.

2. Goals Aligned with the HEART:
To enhance goal achievement, ensure your goals align with your emotions—with your HEART (Healthy, Enduring, Alluring, Relevant, Truth).

3. Purpose and Passion:
Life purpose comprises the fundamental motivating aims of your life, guiding choices, shaping goals, and providing meaning. Passion is discovered through experimentation and finding what truly makes you happy.

4. Finding Your Reasons:
Feeling amazing is not enough; strong reasons related to purpose, identity, and values drive action, especially during life's challenges.

5. Relationship Between Purpose and Passion:
Purpose is about how you relate to others, sharing your unique contributions with the world. Finding your passion involves experimentation, akin to finding true love.

SELF-REFLECTION QUESTIONS

1. SMART Goal Setting:
- How can you apply the SMART criteria to refine and structure your current goals? What adjustments might be needed to make them more specific, measurable, and time-bound?

_____

_____

_____

_____

2. Goals Aligned with the HEART:
   - How well do your current goals align with your emotional well-being and life purpose? In what ways can you make them more enduring, alluring, and relevant to your true self?

_____

_____

_____

_____

3. Purpose and Passion:
   - What aspects of your life reflect your life purpose? How can you experiment to uncover your true, passionate self? In what ways can you align your passions with your life purpose?

_____

_____

_____

_____

4. Finding Your Reasons:
   - What are the reasons behind your current pursuits and goals? How strongly do these reasons connect with your purpose, identity, and values? What adjustments can you make to strengthen your motivations?

_____

_____

_____

_____

_____

_____

5. Relationship Between Purpose and Passion:
- How can you actively integrate your passion into meaningful contributions to others? In what ways does your passion align with your purpose? How does the relationship between your passion and purpose contribute to a sense of fulfillment?

_____

_____

_____

_____

_____

_____

_____

_____

NOTES

CHAPTER 8: ENERGY

FUNDAMENTAL LESSONS

1. Optimal Brain Diet:
   - The brain requires 45 different nutrients for optimal functioning, with some top brain foods including avocados, blueberries, broccoli, dark chocolate, eggs, green leafy vegetables, salmon, turmeric, walnuts, and water.

2. Essential Brain Nutrients:
   - Certain nutrients directly influence cognitive abilities, and obtaining them from real, whole, organic sources is crucial. Consider supplementation with phospholipid DHA, B vitamins, and curcumin for brain health.

3. Exercise for Brain Health:
   - Exercise positively influences the brain, safeguarding memory and thinking skills.

4. Eliminating Automatic Negative Thoughts (ANTS):
   - Identify and replace Automatic Negative Thoughts (ANTS) to promote a positive mindset.

5. Creating a Clean Environment:
   - The quality of the air you breathe directly impacts brain function. Maintain a clean environment in your home and workplace for optimal cognitive performance.

SELF-REFLECTION QUESTIONS

1. Optimal Brain Diet:
   - How can you incorporate these brain-boosting foods into your diet? What adjustments can you make to ensure a nutrient-rich intake for optimal brain health?

_____

_____

_____

_____

2. Essential Brain Nutrients:
Are you conscious of obtaining essential nutrients from your diet? How can you ensure a balanced intake of nutrients crucial for cognitive function?

_____

_____

_____

_____

3. Exercise for Brain Health:
- What forms of exercise do you enjoy? How can you incorporate regular physical activity into your routine to enhance brain health?

_____

_____

_____

_____

4. Eliminating Automatic Negative Thoughts (ANTS):
- What are your most common negative thoughts? How can you challenge and replace them with positive alternatives for mental well-being?

_____

_____

_____

_____

5. Creating a Clean Environment:
- How can you improve the air quality in your living and working spaces? What changes can you make to create a cleaner and healthier environment for your brain?

_____

_____

_____

_____

NOTES

CHAPTER 9: SMALL SIMPLE STEPS

FUNDAMENTAL LESSONS

1. Start with Modest Steps:
   - Take small, simple steps toward your goals—actions that require minimal effort and can be easily incorporated into your routine. These small steps, when repeated, can lead to the formation of habits over time.

2. Behavior Change Factors:
   - According to Dr. Fogg, behavior change can be influenced by having an epiphany, changing your environment, and taking baby steps. Gradual progress is a powerful factor in modifying behavior.

3. Harnessing the Power of Habits:
   - Small, simple steps, when repeated, lead to the formation of habits. A significant portion of daily actions is driven by habits, contributing to automatic behavior.

4. Transforming Life through Basic Behaviors:
   - Significantly altering your life may begin by changing one or two fundamental behaviors. The adoption of new habits, even as simple as brushing your teeth with the opposite hand, can lead to transformative outcomes.

5. Establishing a Morning Routine:
   - Jump-start your day with a morning routine that includes simple tasks. Establishing winning routines early in the day can leverage the science of momentum, making it easier to sustain accomplishments throughout the day.

SELF-REFLECTION QUESTIONS

1. Start with Modest Steps:
   - What are the smallest actions you can take to move closer to your goals? How can you break down your objectives into tiny, manageable steps?

_____

_____

_____

_____

2. Behavior Change Factors:
   - Which of these factors can you apply to facilitate positive changes in your behavior? How can you incorporate baby steps into your daily routine?

_____

_____

_____

_____

3. Harnessing the Power of Habits:
- What habits currently shape your daily life? How can you consciously develop positive habits to automate aspects of your routine?

_____

_____

_____

_____

4. Transforming Life through Basic Behaviors:
- What fundamental behaviors would you like to change or enhance in your life? How can you start with small adjustments that have the potential for a broader impact?

_____

_____

_____

_____

5. Establishing a Morning Routine:
- What morning routine can you create to kickstart your day? How can you use the concept of momentum to build positive energy and productivity?

_____

_____

_____

_____

NOTES

CHAPTER 10: FLOW

FUNDAMENTAL LESSONS

1. Understanding Flow:
   - Flow is a state of optimal experience where individuals are deeply engaged in an activity, finding it enjoyable and rewarding. It is characterized by absolute concentration, a total focus on goals, an altered perception of time, a sense of effortlessness, and comfort with the task at hand.

2. Flow Characteristics:
   - Flow, as defined by Dr. Csikszentmihalyi, exhibits eight characteristics, including absolute concentration, time distortion, a sense of reward, effortlessness, and comfort. Recognizing these features helps in identifying and cultivating the flow state.

3. Finding Flow:
   - Achieving flow involves eliminating distractions, allocating sufficient time, engaging in activities you love, setting clear goals, and challenging yourself moderately. These elements contribute to creating an environment conducive to experiencing flow regularly.

4. Conquering Flow's Adversaries:
   - To reach a state of flow regularly, it's crucial to overcome four supervillains: multitasking, stress, fear of failure, and a lack of conviction. Training yourself to manage these challenges enhances your ability to function at a superhero level.

5. Perfectionism and Creativity:
   - Contrary to popular belief, perfectionism can hinder creativity and innovation. Embracing imperfection and allowing room for mistakes can lead to a more innovative and creative mindset.

SELF-REFLECTION QUESTIONS

1. Understanding Flow:
How often do you experience flow in your daily activities? What are some activities that consistently immerse you in a state of flow?

_____

_____

_____

_____

_____

2. Flow Characteristics:
Which characteristics of flow do you often experience during activities you enjoy? How can you incorporate more flow-inducing activities into your life?

_____

_____

_____

_____

_____

3. Finding Flow:
What distractions hinder your ability to achieve flow? How can you adjust your environment and activities to foster more flow experiences?

_____

_____

_____

_____

_____

4. Conquering Flow's Adversaries:
Which of the flow adversaries do you struggle with the most? How can you develop strategies to conquer these challenges and cultivate a flow mindset?

_____

_____

_____

_____

_____

5. Perfectionism and Creativity:
How does perfectionism manifest in your approach to tasks? In what ways can you embrace imperfection and use it to enhance your creativity?

NOTES

PART IV

LIMITLESS METHODS: THE HOW

CHAPTER 11: FOCUS

FUNDAMENTAL LESSONS

1. Unleashing Superpowers through Focus:
Unlimiting your focus is essential for unlocking your mental superpowers. Complete concentration on a task allows you to achieve levels of performance that are otherwise unattainable when distracted or divided in thought.

2. Eliminating Distractions:
Mastering concentration involves eliminating distractions whenever focus is required. Creating an environment conducive to concentration is crucial for achieving optimal performance and tapping into your mental capabilities.

3. Calming a Busy Mind:
Focus requires the ability to ignore distractions and fully dedicate attention to the task at hand. Practices such as meditation, yoga, and specific breathing exercises, like the 4-7-8 Method, can be effective in calming a busy mind and enhancing concentration.

4. Addressing Stressors:
Identifying and addressing sources of stress is crucial for maintaining concentration. Proactively dealing with stressors and engaging with tasks causing anxiety can contribute to a clearer and more focused mind.

5. Scheduled Time for Distractions:
Designating specific times for distractions can be a practical strategy to manage interruptions without compromising overall focus. By scheduling breaks or allowing time for less demanding activities, you can maintain a balance between focus and relaxation.

SELF-REFLECTION QUESTIONS

1. Unleashing Superpowers through Focus:
* In what areas of your life do you currently experience limitations in focus? How could improving concentration positively impact your performance?

_____

_____

_____

_____

_____

2. Eliminating Distractions:
- What are the primary distractions in your environment? How can you minimize or eliminate these distractions to enhance your ability to concentrate?

_____

_____

_____

_____

3. Calming a Busy Mind:
- Have you tried any mindfulness or relaxation techniques to calm your mind? How might incorporating such practices into your routine improve your ability to focus?

_____

_____

_____

4. Addressing Stressors:
- What tasks or situations cause you stress and hinder your concentration? How can you address or approach these stressors to improve your focus?

_____

_____

_____

5. Scheduled Time for Distractions:
How do you currently manage distractions in your schedule? Can you implement a structured approach to allocate time for breaks and less demanding activities?

_____

_____

_____

_____

NOTES

CHAPTER 12: STUDY

FUNDAMENTAL LESSONS

1. The Four Levels of Competence:
Understanding the four levels of competence—unconscious incompetence, conscious incompetence, conscious competence, and unconscious competence—provides insight into the learning process. Progressing from unawareness to mastery involves self-awareness and active engagement with skills.

2. Lifelong Learning for Success:
Lifelong learning is a hallmark of success. Constantly acquiring new skills and knowledge is essential for personal and professional growth. Successful individuals prioritize continuous learning as a key component of their journey.

3. Effective Study Habits:
Effective studying involves strategies beyond cramming. Quality sleep, focused concentration, and strategic study habits contribute to academic success. Diversifying study techniques, such as active recall, spaced repetition, and sensory engagement, enhances learning outcomes.

4. Sensory Engagement for Memory:
Engaging the senses, including the sense of smell, can enhance memory retention. Using essential oils or other sensory stimuli while studying creates associations that aid recall during exams or when applying learned information.

5. Effective Notetaking Strategies:
Notetaking is a valuable tool for learning, and adopting effective strategies enhances its impact. The TIP mnemonic—Think, Identify, Prioritize—provides a framework for maximizing the benefits of notetaking.

SELF-REFLECTION QUESTIONS

1. The Four Levels of Competence:
In which areas of your life or learning journey do you currently identify with each level of competence? How can you move toward greater self-awareness and competence?

_____

_____

_____

_____

_____

2. Lifelong Learning for Success:
What skills or subjects are you currently interested in learning or improving? How can you incorporate a mindset of lifelong learning into your daily life?

_____

_____

_____

_____

3. Effective Study Habits:
What study habits do you currently employ? How might incorporating active recall, spaced repetition, and sensory engagement improve your study sessions?

_____

_____

_____

_____

4. Sensory Engagement for Memory:
Have you explored sensory engagement in your study routine? How might incorporating scents or other sensory elements positively impact your memory?

_____

_____

_____

_____

5. Effective Notetaking Strategies:
How do you approach notetaking in your learning process? Can you apply the TIP mnemonic to improve the quality and relevance of your notes?

_____

_____

_____

_____

NOTES

CHAPTER 13: MEMORY

FUNDAMENTAL LESSONS

1. Memory is Like a Muscle:
   * The brain, like a muscle, requires consistent exercise to stay fit. The use-it-or-lose-it principle applies, and intentional efforts to keep the mind active and engaged are essential for maintaining cognitive fitness.

2. Memory is a Vital Component:
   * Memory is integral to various aspects of brain function, and upgrading your brain involves unlimiting your memory. Recognizing the significance of memory in daily life emphasizes the need for memory enhancement strategies.

3. Trained vs. Untrained Memory:
   * There is no inherent "good" or "bad" memory; instead, memory can be trained or untrained. Shifting from a fixed mindset about memory to recognizing its trainable nature empowers individuals to enhance their memory.

4. MOM Approach for Instant Memory Kick-Up:
   * The MOM approach—Motivation, Observation, Methods—provides a framework for instantly boosting memory. Aligning motivation, improving observation skills, and employing effective memory methods contribute to enhanced recall.

5. Effective Memory Enhancement Techniques:
   * Utilizing effective memory enhancement techniques, such as association, active learning, visualization, emotion, and location, significantly improves memory retention. Creating meaningful associations, engaging in active learning, visualizing information, infusing emotion, and leveraging spatial memory contribute to better recall.

SELF-REFLECTION QUESTIONS

1. Memory is Like a Muscle:
   * In what ways do you currently exercise your brain? How might you incorporate more mental activities and challenges into your daily routine?

_____

_____

_____

_____

_____

2. Memory is a Vital Component:
- How has your awareness of the importance of memory evolved? What steps can you take to actively improve and unlimit your memory?

_____

_____

_____

_____

3. Trained vs. Untrained Memory:
- How do you perceive your own memory abilities? In what ways can you adopt a more growth-oriented and trainable mindset toward memory?

_____

_____

_____

_____

4. MOM Approach for Instant Memory Kick-Up:
- How can you integrate the MOM approach into situations where memory recall is crucial? What motivations can you leverage to enhance memory performance?

_____

_____

_____

_____

5. Effective Memory Enhancement Techniques:
- Which memory enhancement techniques resonate with you? How can you incorporate these techniques into your learning and daily life for improved memory?

_____

_____

_____

_____

NOTES

CHAPTER 14: SPEED READING

FUNDAMENTAL LESSONS

1. Reading and Success Connection:
Studies establish a direct correlation between reading ability and overall success in life. Reading enhances memory, focus, vocabulary, imagination, and understanding, contributing to cognitive development and success.

2. Benefits of Reading:
Reading makes the brain limitless by positively impacting memory, focus, vocabulary, imagination, and comprehension. Recognizing the multifaceted benefits of reading highlights its role as a cognitive enhancer.

3. Hurdles to Faster Reading:
Three obstacles to reading faster are regression, outdated skills, and subvocalization. Identifying and addressing these hurdles are crucial steps toward improving reading speed and efficiency.

4. Dispelling Reading Myths:
Common myths about reading speed, comprehension, and appreciation are debunked. Faster readers can comprehend well, reading faster requires less effort, and fast readers can appreciate the reading experience.

5. Strategies for Faster Reading:
To read even faster, employ strategies like expanding peripheral vision and minimizing subvocalization. Treating reading as a skill to be developed, similar to working out, helps strengthen "reading muscles" and improve reading speed.

SELF-REFLECTION QUESTIONS

1. Reading and Success Connection:
• How has your reading habit influenced various aspects of your life? In what ways can you further leverage reading to enhance your success?

_____

_____

_____

_____

_____

2. Benefits of Reading:
• Which specific benefits of reading resonate with you, and how have you experienced these enhancements in your own life?

_____

_____

_____

_____

_____

3. Hurdles to Faster Reading:
Which of these hurdles do you find most challenging in your reading practice?
How can you overcome or minimize these obstacles?

_____

_____

_____

_____

4. Dispelling Reading Myths:
Have you held any of these myths about reading speed? How can dispelling
these myths positively impact your approach to reading?

_____

_____

_____

_____

5. Strategies for Faster Reading:
What strategies resonate with you for increasing your reading speed? How can
you incorporate these strategies into your reading routine to enhance
efficiency?

_____

_____

_____

_____

NOTES

CHAPTER 15: THINKING

FUNDAMENTAL LESSONS

1. Diversity of Intelligences:
Embrace the idea that intelligence is not a singular entity but comes in various forms. Howard Gardner's theory identifies eight distinct intelligences, including spatial, bodily-kinesthetic, musical, linguistic, logical-mathematical, interpersonal, intrapersonal, and naturalistic.

2. Personalized Learning Styles:
Understand your learning style by identifying whether you are a Visual, Auditory, or Kinesthetic learner (VAK). This knowledge helps tailor your learning experiences to align with your preferred mode of information processing.

3. Visual Learning (V):
Visual learners grasp information best through visual aids such as charts, illustrations, and videos. Leveraging visual elements enhances their comprehension and retention of information.

4. Auditory Learning (A):
Auditory learners excel in learning through listening, whether it's lectures, discussions, podcasts, or audiobooks. Engaging their auditory senses optimizes their learning process.

5. Kinesthetic Learning (K):
Kinesthetic learners thrive in hands-on learning experiences. Physical interaction and tactile engagement contribute significantly to their understanding and retention of information.

SELF-REFLECTION QUESTIONS

1. Diversity of Intelligences:
Which of these intelligences do you resonate with the most? How can recognizing diverse intelligences contribute to a richer understanding of human capabilities?

---

2. Personalized Learning Styles:
Reflect on your dominant learning style (Visual, Auditory, or Kinesthetic).
How has understanding your learning style influenced your approach to
acquiring new knowledge?

_____

_____

_____

_____

3. Visual Learning (V):
In what ways have visual aids proven effective in your learning experiences?
How can you incorporate more visual elements into your study or work
routines?

_____

_____

_____

_____

4. Auditory Learning (A):
How often do you incorporate auditory learning methods into your routine?
What benefits have you observed when learning through auditory channels?

_____

_____

_____

_____

5. Kinesthetic Learning (K):
How can you incorporate more kinesthetic learning activities into your
educational or professional pursuits? What hands-on experiences have proven
most effective for you in the past?

_____

_____

_____

_____

_____

NOTES

PART V

LIMITLESS MOMENTUM: THE WHEN

CHAPTER 16: LIMITLESS AT WORK

FUNDAMENTAL LESSONS

1. Importance of Emotional Intelligence (EQ):
   - Understand the significance of emotional intelligence in the workplace for effective collaboration, self-management, and leadership.

2. Mindfulness for Presence:
   - Recognize the role of mindfulness in staying present at work. Consider how being present can positively impact your performance and relationships.

3. Empowering Questions:
   - Learn the power of asking empowering questions in the workplace. Understand how thoughtful questioning can contribute to personal and professional growth.

4. Scheduling Flow Time:
   - Acknowledge the value of scheduling dedicated "flow time" for highly productive and focused work. Explore how creating optimal conditions can enhance your performance.

5. Continuous Learning and Purpose Alignment:
   - Emphasize the importance of continuous learning, contributing to the workplace, and staying aligned with your purpose. Reflect on how these elements contribute to a limitless approach to work.

SELF-REFLECTION QUESTIONS

1. Emotional Intelligence (EQ):
How would you rate your current level of emotional intelligence in the workplace? In what ways can you enhance your ability to understand and manage your emotions, as well as those of others?

_____

_____

_____

_____

_____

2. Mindfulness and Presence:
Reflect on a recent work situation where mindfulness and being present could have positively impacted the outcome. How can you incorporate mindfulness practices into your daily work routine?

_____

_____

_____

_____

_____

3. Empowering Questions:

Consider a recent challenge or opportunity at work. What empowering questions could you ask yourself or others to gain insights, solutions, or a new perspective on the situation?

_____

_____

_____

_____

4. Scheduling Flow Time:

Assess your current work schedule. Do you allocate dedicated "flow time" for focused and highly productive work? How can you optimize your schedule to create more conducive conditions for flow?

_____

_____

_____

_____

5. Continuous Learning and Purpose Alignment:

Reflect on your approach to continuous learning at work. How do you contribute to the workplace, and does it align with your sense of purpose? Identify one action to enhance your commitment to learning and purposeful contribution.

_____

_____

_____

_____

NOTES

CHAPTER 17: UNDERSTANDING YOUR BRAIN ANIMAL C.O.D.E.

FUNDAMENTAL LESSONS

1. Individual Brain Types:
Recognize that individuals have unique brain types, represented as the Agile Cheetah, Wise Owl, Creative Dolphin, and Empathetic Elephant. Each type comes with its own strengths and weaknesses.

2. Cheetah Strengths:
For Agile Cheetahs, harness the power of quick thinking and adaptability. Set short-term goals, engage in hands-on experiences, and practice time management techniques like time blocking.

3. Cheetah Weaknesses and Improvement:
Cheetahs can improve by cultivating patience, enhancing planning skills, and actively listening to others. Focus on preparation to avoid unnecessary mistakes and gather valuable insights from different perspectives.

4. Owl Strengths:
Wise Owls excel in logical thinking, attention to detail, and analytical skills. Create clear plans, establish structured routines, and engage in logic puzzles to enhance learning and problem-solving.

5. Owl Weaknesses and Improvement:
Improve emotional intelligence, communication skills, and adaptability. Recognize the importance of emotions in decision-making, seek feedback from others, and embrace flexibility in the face of change.

6. Dolphin Strengths:
Creative Dolphins are visionaries with strong intuition and out-of-the-box thinking. Enhance creativity through engaging in artistic activities, maintaining a stimulating environment, and practicing mindfulness exercises.

7. Dolphin Weaknesses and Improvement:
Develop organizational skills to add structure to creative processes. Sharpen analytical skills to prioritize tasks effectively and avoid chasing impractical ideas. Learn to balance creativity with planning.

8. Elephant Strengths:
Empathetic Elephants excel in emotional intelligence and collaboration. Strengthen communication skills, participate in group activities, and delegate tasks based on team members' strengths.

9. Elephant Weaknesses and Improvement:
Improve decision-making when consensus isn't possible. Practice working independently to trust personal instincts, assert oneself, and make confident decisions. Balance collaboration with the ability to lead.

10. Balanced Approach:
Strive for a balanced and effective approach to work, learning, and personal growth by leveraging the strengths of your brain type and addressing areas for improvement. Embrace a growth mindset and continuous self-awareness.

SELF-REFLECTION QUESTIONS

1. Understanding Your Brain Type:
   • Reflect on the idea that individuals have unique brain types. Which animal type—Cheetah, Owl, Dolphin, or Elephant—do you identify with the most, and why?

_____

_____

_____

_____

2. Cheetah Strengths:
   • How can you harness quick thinking and adaptability in your daily life? What are some short-term goals you can set to enhance your productivity?

_____

_____

_____

_____

_____

3. Cheetah Weaknesses and Improvement:
   • What specific planning skills can you work on to enhance your efficiency? In what situations can you actively listen to others to gain valuable insights?

_____

_____

_____

_____

_____

4. Owl Strengths:
- How can you use logical thinking and attention to detail to create clearer plans?

_____

_____

_____

_____

- What structured routines can you establish to improve your focus?

_____

_____

_____

_____

5. Owl Weaknesses and Improvement:
- In what ways can you enhance your communication skills and seek feedback?

_____

_____

_____

_____

6. Dolphin Strengths:
- How can you engage in creative endeavors to enhance innovative thinking? What elements can you incorporate into your workspace to promote creativity?

_____

_____

_____

_____

7. Dolphin Weaknesses and Improvement:
How can you add more structure to your creative processes? In what ways can analytical skills help you prioritize tasks effectively?

_____

_____

_____

_____

8. Elephant Strengths:
  • How can you further strengthen your communication skills?

_____

_____

_____

_____

  • What group activities can you participate in to enhance collaboration?

_____

_____

9. Elephant Weaknesses and Improvement:
  • How can you make confident decisions when consensus isn't possible?

_____

_____

_____

_____

  • In what ways can you practice working independently to trust your instincts?

_____

_____

_____

_____

_____

10. Balanced Approach:
- How will you strive for a balanced and effective approach to work, learning, and personal growth?

_____

_____

_____

_____

_____

- In what areas can you embrace a growth mindset for continuous self-awareness and improvement?

_____

_____

_____

_____

- How can you apply the strengths of your brain type while addressing areas that need improvement?

_____

_____

_____

_____

_____

NOTES

CHAPTER 18: BRAIN NUTRITION

FUNDAMENTAL LESSONS

1. Genetics vs. Lifestyle: Contrary to the myth that "brain health is all about genetics," it's crucial to recognize the significant impact of lifestyle choices, especially diet, on brain health and cognitive function. A nutritious diet can play a key role in preventing cognitive decline and enhancing mental function.

2. Diverse Understanding of Fats: Challenge the misconception that "all fats are bad for the brain" and understand the importance of healthy fats, such as omega-3 fatty acids found in foods like fish, walnuts, and flaxseeds. These fats are essential for brain function and cell maintenance.

3. Quality Over Quantity: Dispel the myth that "eating enough ensures all the nutrients your brain needs." Emphasize the importance of the quality of food consumed, highlighting that a diverse and nutrient-dense diet is essential for providing the brain with the necessary nutrients for optimal function.

4. Multivitamins vs. Whole Foods: Address the misconception that "taking a multivitamin is enough to cover all your brain's nutritional needs." While multivitamins can address deficiencies, emphasize that they should complement, not replace, a nutritious diet rich in whole foods.

5. Sugar and Cognitive Health: Challenge the idea that "the more sugar, the better for the brain." Acknowledge that while the brain uses glucose for energy, not all sugars are equal. Excessive consumption of refined sugars can lead to metabolic disruptions and inflammation. Encourage a diet rich in complex carbohydrates from whole grains and vegetables for a consistent and healthy glucose supply.

SELF-REFLECTION QUESTIONS

1. Genetics and Lifestyle: Reflect on your understanding of the interplay between genetics and lifestyle in determining brain health. How has this insight influenced your perception of personal responsibility for cognitive well-being?

_____

_____

_____

_____

_____

2. Healthy Fats: Consider your dietary habits regarding fat consumption. Are you conscious of incorporating sources of healthy fats into your meals? How might integrating omega-3 fatty acids into your diet positively impact your brain health?

_____

_____

_____

_____

3. Quality of Nutrition: Assess the quality of your nutritional choices. How diverse and nutrient-dense is your typical diet? In what ways can you enhance the nutritional value of your meals to better support your brain function?

_____

_____

_____

_____

4. Multivitamins and Whole Foods: Examine your approach to nutritional supplements, especially multivitamins. Do you see them as a complement or a replacement for whole foods? How can you strike a balance between supplement use and prioritizing a rich, whole-food-based diet?

_____

_____

_____

_____

5. Sugar Awareness: Reflect on your awareness of sugar consumption and its sources in your diet. Are you mindful of the types of sugars you consume? How can you adjust your diet to provide your brain with a more consistent and healthy supply of glucose?

_____

_____

_____

_____

_____

NOTES

CHAPTER 19: HOW ARTIFITIAL INTELLIGENCE CAN ENHANCE HUMAN INTELLIGENCE

FUNDAMENTAL LESSONS

1. AI as a Complementary Tool: Recognize that the true power of AI lies in its role as a complementary tool, enhancing your cognitive abilities rather than replacing them. Think of yourself as the skilled artisan, with AI as a tool to amplify your capabilities.

2. Avoiding Doomsday Scenarios: Dispel the notion of AI replacing humans as portrayed in doomsday scenarios like Skynet. Embrace the idea that AI is designed to assist and collaborate with us, not to take over our roles. The objective is to improve task performance, not relinquish control.

3. AI Redefined as Augmented Intelligence: Shift your perspective on AI by redefining it as Augmented Intelligence rather than Artificial Intelligence. Understand that augmentation involves enhancing and making something better, emphasizing how AI can elevate our innate skills and talents.

4. Personalization and Customization: Learn from Sam's journey and understand the value of personalization in AI applications. Customized learning plans, adaptive testing, and understanding individual preferences are crucial in maximizing the benefits of AI, tailoring its assistance to individual needs.

5. Synergy between Human Drive and AI: Sam's success story illustrates the synergy between personal determination and AI assistance. Recognize that AI is a powerful tool, but its effectiveness is amplified when combined with human drive, curiosity, and a commitment to learning and growth. The true potential emerges when we skillfully integrate AI into our pursuits.

SELF-REFLECTION QUESTIONS

1. AI as a Complementary Tool:
   - How do you currently view the role of AI in your life? Do you see it as a complementary tool or more as a replacement for certain tasks?

_____

_____

_____

_____

_____

- In what aspects of your work or daily activities do you think AI could enhance your cognitive abilities and productivity?

_____

_____

_____

_____

2. Avoiding Doomsday Scenarios:
- Reflect on your perceptions of AI, especially those influenced by media portrayals or fictional scenarios. How can you shift your mindset to see AI as a collaborator rather than a potential threat?

_____

_____

_____

_____

- Are there specific tasks or areas where you've been hesitant to embrace AI? What steps can you take to approach these with a more open mindset?

_____

_____

_____

_____

3. AI Redefined as Augmented Intelligence:
- Consider the concept of Augmented Intelligence. How does this perspective change your understanding of AI's role in enhancing human abilities?

_____

_____

_____

_____

- In what areas of your life or work do you believe AI could augment your skills and talents to achieve better outcomes?

_____

_____

_____

_____

4. Personalization and Customization:
- Reflect on the importance of personalization in AI applications. How tailored are the tools and technologies you currently use to your individual preferences and needs?

_____

_____

_____

_____

- Can you identify areas where personalized AI assistance could significantly improve your learning, productivity, or overall well-being?

_____

_____

_____

_____

5. Synergy between Human Drive and AI:
- Think about instances in your life where your determination and drive have led to success. How might AI enhance or support these efforts?

_____

_____

_____

_____

- How can you proactively integrate AI into your learning and growth journey, following the example of Sam, to achieve more significant and efficient results?

_____

_____

_____

_____

6. Balancing Control and Assistance:
- Evaluate your comfort level with relinquishing control to AI in certain tasks. Are there areas where you could benefit from allowing AI to assist more actively?

_____

_____

_____

_____

- Consider situations where AI might not be the most suitable assistant. How can you strike a balance between utilizing AI and relying on your own expertise?

_____

_____

_____

_____

NOTES

AUTHOR

Dear Reader,

I wanted to take a moment to express my heartfelt gratitude for your recent purchase. It was an absolute pleasure serving you, and I hope that this 'workbook' exceeded your expectations.

Your support means the world to me, and I greatly value your satisfaction. If you have a spare moment, I would truly appreciate it if you could share your experience by leaving a review or rating. Your feedback not only helps me improve but also assists other customers in making informed decisions.

I strive to provide exceptional workbooks, and your opinion is invaluable to me. Please visit the product page to share your thoughts.

Once again, thank you for choosing me. I look forward to serving you in the future and exceeding your expectations.

Warmest regards,

Jada J. Carlson

Made in the USA
Coppell, TX
17 February 2025